Fred was going to have a bonfire.
He pushed the leaves into a pile.

Tessa and Tony saw the pile of leaves.
'Look, Tony,' said Tessa.

Tessa ran to the pile of leaves and jumped over it.
'I did it,' said Tessa.
'I jumped over the pile of leaves.'

Tony looked at the pile of leaves.
'I will get over it too,' he said.

Tony ran and jumped over the pile of leaves.
'I did it too,' said Tony.
'I jumped over the pile of leaves.'

Kevin saw Tony and Tessa.
Kevin had a bag of chips.

'We jumped over the pile of leaves,' said Tessa.
'You could not get over it,' said Tony.

'I could,' said Kevin. 'Look.'

Kevin ran and jumped over the pile of leaves, but he dropped his chips.

Kevin was cross.
'Look,' said Kevin.
'I have dropped all my chips in the leaves.'

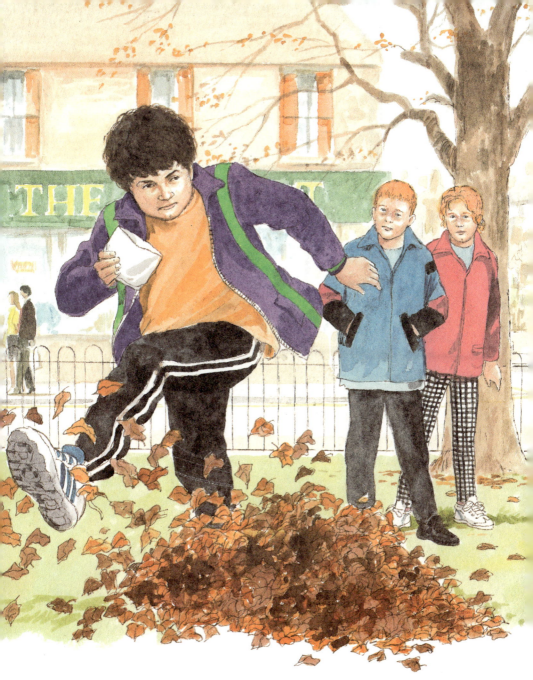

Kevin kicked the pile of leaves.

Fred was putting leaves into his bag.
He saw the children.
Fred was cross.
'Who kicked over my pile of leaves?' he said.

Fred looked at Kevin.
'Did you kick my leaves?' he said.
'No,' said Kevin.
'It was Tony.
He kicked the leaves.'

'It was not,' said Tessa.
'Tony did not kick the leaves.'
Fred looked in the leaves.
'Who dropped chips in my leaves?'
he said to Kevin.

'You have the bag, Kevin.
It was you!
You dropped the chips
and you kicked my leaves!'

Fred and Kevin made a bonfire out of leaves
... and chips!